The Fragrance of Love

Dan & Dave Davidson

New Leaf Press

First printing: November 2001

ISBN: 0-89221-509-7
Library of Congress Catalog Number: 2001092041

Photos by Dave Davidson
Illustrations by Nancy G. Daniel

Printed in the United States of America

Please visit our website for other great titles:
www.newleafpress.net

For information regarding publicity for author
interviews contact Dianna Fletcher at (870) 438-5288.

Presented to:

_____

Presented by:

_____

Date:

_____

There is something special about the fragile and momentary beautiful bloom of a flower. Its exclusive fragrance is a blessing for those who dare and care to notice it, just as God intended love to be shared.

With nature being a gift from God, it's a natural response for flower bouquets to be exchanged by couples in love. After discovering God's ultimate definition of love found in 1 Corinthians 13 and knowing His true gifts, there's a field full of meaningful reflections of love's journey from passionate dreams to lasting commitments.

This is the fragrance of love. . . . Whatever goes into nurturing the seed, making it grow, and sustaining its health is part of creating the scent of a shared blessing, not just for two but for all who are near.

We dedicate this book to our wives, Kim and Joan, as we share our reflections with you. Take time to smell the roses and may God bless you in the garden of your love relationships.

— Dan & Dave Davidson

Contents

Gardener's Delight

AWAKE, NORTH WIND, AND COME, SOUTH WIND!
BLOW ON MY GARDEN, THAT ITS FRAGRANCE MAY SPREAD
ABROAD. LET MY LOVER COME INTO HIS GARDEN AND TASTE
ITS CHOICE FRUITS.   *Song of Solomon 4:16*

Some flowers bloom for only a short time. Their colors seem to vanish as quickly as they had burst forth in glory. To some, love is the same. It seems to leave suddenly after its first wave of passion.

In the eyes of a seasoned gardener though, there is much more to life than the peak blossom of spring. There is joy in planting, in growing, and in the nurturing of new life. True, committed love is much the same.

The patience of a gardener helps to produce beauty beyond description. Patience can also help create an abiding love that words cannot express. When planted in deep rich soil, love relationships are nourished and sustained by the Master Gardener, God himself.

Dan Davidson

What better place
for a man to kneel down
and offer a kiss, a ring, or a
hand, than amongst the flowers
and foliage of a garden path leading
to an ornate gazebo.

Dave Davidson

THERE IS JUST AS MUCH BEAUTY VISIBLE TO US IN THE LANDSCAPE
AS WE ARE PREPARED TO APPRECIATE – NOT A GRAIN MORE.

Henry David Thoreau

The Almighty Creator,
having a heart of a faithful father,
bestows His very finest handiwork
upon those who simply notice.

Dave Davidson

GOD CREATED THE FIRST MAN AND WOMAN,
ADAM AND EVE, AND CHOSE A BEAUTIFUL SETTING
FOR THEM TO SHARE THEIR LOVE TOGETHER
— A GARDEN.

Dan Davidson

The garden will never be finished,
but that adds to the pleasure.

Robert Meltzer

'TIS TRULY AMAZING THAT SUCH BEAUTY EMERGES FROM THE GROUND . . .
EACH BLADE OF GRASS, A RECKONING;
EACH FLOWER PETAL, EVIDENCE OF A
MASTER GARDENER METHODICALLY MAKING MINI-MIRACLES.

Dave Davidson

In his garden every man may be his own artist
without apology or explanation.
Here is one spot where each may experience
the "romance of possibility."

Louise Beebe Wilder

9

A rendezvous planned,
just before sunset at the wooden bridge.
Walking along a cobblestone path
winding around the lake,
the pink, purple, and lavender
wildflower blossoms
for a moment
take my breath away,
much like your love and devotion
which cause me to stop
and sigh quietly
many times in the day.

Dan Davidson

Comfort of Friendship

Perfume and incense bring joy to the heart, and the pleasantness of one's friend springs from his earnest counsel. *Proverbs 27:9*

At the foundation of love lies friendship. The deepest love shared between two people is built on more than feelings; it is strong and enduring because of the nourishing roots of friendship and commitment. Friends give grace and are more apt to overlook faults and quirks in our personalities. A true friend's love is unconditional, which can be a needed source of comfort and acceptance in a sometimes lonely world.

A relationship without friendship is not likely to endure the storms of life. For love to last, it must first be shared among friends.

Dan Davidson

Love anything and your heart will be wrung and possibly broken. If you want to make sure of keeping it intact you must give it to no one, not even an animal. Wrap it carefully round with hobbies and little luxuries; avoid all entanglements. Lock it up safe in the casket or coffin of your selfishness. But in that casket — safe, dark, motionless, airless — it will change. It will not be broken; it will become unbreakable, impenetrable, irredeemable. To **love is** to be vulnerable.

C.S. Lewis

LOVE IS FRIENDSHIP SET ON FIRE.

Jeremy Taylor

Love is

in its very essence . . . liberty:
it is compatible neither with
obedience, jealousy, nor fear:
it is . . . most pure, perfect, and
unlimited where its votaries live in
confidence, equality, and unreserve.

Percy Bysshe Shelley

We always believe our first **love is**
our last, and our last love our first.

George Whyte-Melville

Only when a heart is willing to be broken,

can true love begin to be revealed. By sharing

a secret or personal story close to the heart, a transparency

challenges the comfort of friendship in a relationship.

When a heart is vulnerable in the arms of someone

it loves, the foundation for a deep and lasting

bond is created. It's that moment of comfort

or consolation, which exclaims "I am here

for you when you need me."

Dan & Dave Davidson

Passionate Romance

FOR LOVE IS AS STRONG AS DEATH, ITS JEALOUSY UNYIELDING AS THE GRAVE. IT BURNS LIKE BLAZING FIRE; LIKE A MIGHTY FLAME. MANY WATERS CANNOT QUENCH LOVE; RIVERS CANNOT WASH IT AWAY. *Song of Solomon 8:6–7*

A passionate heart knows where its love belongs. It knows where the well holds water and where red carpets unravel. One is willing to walk anywhere with the one he loves, dreaming of the day when the weary head can rest against the shoulders of his chosen beloved and let that passion ignite right in God's sight. It longs for a chance to slow dance. It smirks at patience while trying to peek ahead to the next hour, until two hearts be one.

A passionate heart is semi-desperate, multi-creative, and mildly wild to the touch. Attraction struggles to drive intention in a journey of priorities. Sincere romantic love balances the teeter-totter of infatuation and discourages distraction to fulfill love's potential. Passion serves its purpose and is called upon anytime a heart in love needs resuscitation.

Dave Davidson

To **love is** to admire with the heart; to admire is to love with the mind. *Gautier*

THE HIDDEN RISK IN **LOVE IS** LIKE WALKING A TIGHTROPE OVER NIAGARA FALLS OR WADING KNEE HIGH, KISSING IN A COUNTRY STREAM. IT'S THE FEAR OF HEIGHTS MIXED WITH A COOL QUENCHING OF LOVE'S DELICATE DESIRE.

Dave Davidson

Love is a kiss rekindling; just as sticks rub together —
sparks fly, flames arise, warmth is nurtured,
passion created. *Dave Davidson*

Romance is the icing,
but **love is** the cake.

Unknown

Kisses kept are wasted;
love is to be tasted.

E. V. Cooke

Love is kindest,
and hath most strength,
The kisses are most sweet,
When it's enjoyed in heat of strength,
Where like affections meet.

Patrick Hannay

Dreams Discovered

The best things in life are never quite as rewarding without someone who intimately cares for us sharing our joy. Fulfillment is heightened when a loved one understands our dreams and joins us in the celebrations of life.

God gives us each the desires of His heart. Often, the discovery of lifelong godly ambitions is reflected and revealed when two people in love journey together on a common path.

Dreams that were once stored secretly in the heart become intertwined with the dreams of another. As love grows over the years, the dreams of two meld into one. That is when we realize that to love together is to dream together.

Dan Davidson

"I had a dream! I had a dream!"

Jeremiah 23:25

19

Love is
the most terrible,
and also the most generous
of all the passions; it is the only
one which includes in the dreams
the happiness of someone else.

Alphone Karr

Love is friendship set to music. *Robert Pollok*

LOVE IS BUT THE DISCOVERY OF OURSELVES IN
OTHERS, AND THE DELIGHT IN THE RECOGNITION.

Alexander Smith

The fate of **love is**
that it always seems
too little or too much.

Amelia Barr

Dreams are not to be broadcast to the world,
but rather kept safe in the secret places of the heart.
*To share **love is** to discover another's dreams,*
an intimate exchange of trust and hope.

Dan Davidson

Love is composed of a single soul
inhabiting two bodies.

Helen Hayes

21

LOVE IS DREAMY AND DARING, DANGEROUS
AND DELICATE, COMFORTABLE AND CAUTIOUS,
INTRICATE AND INTIMATE.

Dave Davidson

Love is
discovering a new side
of yourself while sharing
the shadow of another.

Dave Davidson

Love is when a person's . . . own boundary expands
to include you, the other, that was previously outside himself.

Frederick S. Peris

Love is the
result, reflex,
reward, reprise;
the recipe, reverie,
reception, reverence
refining, reflection;
the refreshment,
and responsibly,
the reinvestment,
and resemblance;
the rejuvenation,
and revelation
of even greater love.

Dave Davidson

LOVE IS THE MOOD OF BELIEVING IN MIRACLES.

John C. Powys

Love is
an attempt to
change a piece of the
dream world into reality.

Theodore Roethke

Love is
when you look at the
simple and ordinary things
in life and see beauty.

Dan Davidson

To be in **love is** the dearest wish, the most welcoming
dream and brightest aspiration a heart can hope for.

Becca Lynn

LOVE IS AN IRRESISTIBLE DESIRE TO BE IRRESISTIBLY DESIRED.

Robert Frost

Flustered & Foolish

A heart flustered is a unique creature floating, drifting, and sailing uncharted courses. It's full of passion and frequently foolish, yet frightened by its potential strength. It questions each and every move it makes, evaluating each new feeling, playing the game of second-guessing. The answers which emerge tend to baffle, befuddle, and bewilder the heart, which only spurs on more foolishness.

A heart flustered is constantly on edge, battling faith and fate in a cruel duel, seeking love's final victory. Only with the peace of passing time will true love sign treaty with the flustered heart. This is when freedom begins and love's fighting war is won.   *Dave Davidson*

THEN DELILAH SAID TO SAMSON,
"YOU HAVE MADE A FOOL OF ME"
Judges 16:10.

LOVE IS — DESIRING TO GIVE WHAT IS OUR OWN TO
ANOTHER AND FEELING HIS DELIGHT AS OUR OWN.

Robert A. Heinlein & Emanuel Swedenborg

The heart that loves is always young. *Unknown*

Love is the wisdom of the fool
and the folly of the wise.

Samuel Johnson

I used to check off
my list to see what I missed
. . . looking for hearts off a grocery list.
I'm not too sure what **love is** anymore.

Matt Malyon

Love is a second life; it grows into the soul, warms every vein, and beats in every pulse.

Joseph Addison

TO **LOVE IS** TO CHOOSE. *Joseph Roux*

It may be a nature scene, rolling hills, grass that's green . . . Beauty is a mysterious thing; opens my eyes, makes me sing.

Dave Davidson

All **love is** sweet, given or returned. They who inspire it are fortunate, but those who feel it most are happier still.

Percy Shelley

Love is
most nearly itself
when here and now
cease to matter.

T.S. Eliot

Love is the only gold.
Tennyson

Love is a mutual
misunderstanding.
Oscar Wilde

Love is sentimental
measles.

Charles Kingsley

Love is
the beginning,
the middle,
and the end of
everything.
Jean B. Lacordaire

Love is not love until love's vulnerable.

Theodore Roethke

LOVE IS NOT AN EMPTINESS LONGING TO BE FILLED —
IT IS A FULLNESS PRESSING TO BE RELEASED. *J. Kennedy Shultz*

Where **love is** concerned,
too much is not even enough.

Pierre-Augustin de Beaumarchais

Love is a mystery which,
when solved, evaporates.

Ned Noren

Love is a capricious creature which desires everything and
can be contented with almost nothing.

Madeline de Scudery

29

Laughter & Love

Long after the mountain peaks of passion have risen and fallen, abiding love is perhaps best expressed when lovers share laughter and have fun together in the simple moments of life. A growing repertoire of inside jokes that only two understand strengthens a love based on shared experiences. Whether found in a spontaneous giggle or a reassuring smile, laughter and joy always make love grow.

A mature and genuine love can take a misunderstanding in the morning and turn it into healthy fun by the end of the day. Laughter heals and comforts the unintended blunders in relationships. Laughter and love are truly good for the heart, like good medicine. *Dan Davidson*

Love is a dictionary and thesaurus
with the pages all glued together. *Hugh Myrrh*

Love is a fan club with
only two fans.

Adrian Henri

LOVE IS A CANDLELIGHT DINNER ABOARD A SPEEDBOAT. *Hugh Myrrh*

***Love is** simultaneously proper
nutrition and a delectable dessert.*

Dave Davidson

LOVE IS A CONFLICT BETWEEN REFLEXES AND REFLECTIONS.

Magnus Hirschfeld

31

LOVE IS EITHER A SLAP IN THE FACE
OR A KISS ON THE CHEEK.

Dave Davidson

Love is
heartburn
without the
chili.

Hugh Myrrh

Love is
a gross
exaggeration
of the difference
between one person
and everybody else.

George Bernard Shaw

Poetic Portrait

Poetry and art share the distinct privileges of attempting to capture the many portraits of the beautiful and even the heartbreaking aspects of love's spectrum. Descriptions and reflections become the paints and hues of a love story's picture caught like a photo's print.

When a heart is first in love, it lays a canvas for the whole relationship.

This is the time for foreshadowing to form foundations, for strolls in the park and other delightful memories to make the bonds of lasting solid structures. The changing seasons warn and beckon those falling in love. It's time to make a difference, to cherish your moments, to play outdoors, to kiss more, to listen closer, to make the time together count, making life more memorable.

Dave Davidson

You who dwell in the gardens with friends in attendance,
let me hear your voice! *Song of Solomon 8:13*

Love is a canvas
furnished by nature and
embroidered by imagination.

Voltaire

LOVE IS A GRACIOUS AND BEAUTIFUL ART.

Havelock Ellis

Falling in **love is** drowning in your deepest thoughts.
Nothing else matters, except your wonderful love.

Petrarch

Love is transparent,
yet full of color;
a reflecting rainbow
that cannot be held.

Dave Davidson

Perfect **love is** rare indeed. . . . To be a lover will require that you continually have the subtlety of the very wise, the flexibility of the child, the sensitivity of the artist, the understanding of the philosopher, the acceptance of the saint, the tolerance of the scholar, and the fortitude of the certain.

Leo Buscaglia

Love is the passion of hearts, the language of poetry and the entertainment of drama mixed with the mystery of fiction. *Dave Davidson*

FALLING IN **LOVE IS** SOMETHING YOU FORGET, LIKE PAIN.

Nina Bawden

Love is a mirror that reveals secrets, refines perception, and reflects reality into romance.

Dave Davidson

Love is

in the poetry, the music, the flowers,

the perfume, the dancing, the moonlight sky,

the slow burning fire, the shimmering dresses,

the smoothest of men, the eye-batting beauty,

the ocean by morning, the tender kisses at night,

the long, flowing tendrils, the way he says my name,

the mountains in winter, the sunset's water

reflection. All these possibilities feed your

romantic spirit and keep it alive.

Becca Lynn

Awakened Senses

How delightful is your love, my sister, my bride! How much more pleasing is
your love than wine, and the fragrance of your perfume than any spice!

Song of Solomon 4:10

Love has a way of awakening our senses like nothing else in life. There
comes a time to take the next step, to open the heart
in a new way is risky. At that moment, the journey of
love can seem truly unpredictable. Rational responses
of the mind can be replaced by impulsive decisions
prompted by flutters in the stomach.

When love is first born, our senses are heightened to new levels. We pause to hear birds singing at sunrise
and each sunset is a new miracle to behold. Flowers bloom
in vivid colors that went unnoticed before. Life is
indeed sweeter when love is in the air!

Dan Davidson

Love is of all the passions the strongest, for it attacks simultaneously the head, the heart, and the senses.

Voltaire

Love is that condition in which the happiness of another person is essential to your own joy.

George Eliot

Love is a great beautifier.

Louisa May Alcott

Love is to stop comparing.

Bernard Grasset

Love is at first sight only realizing an imagination that has always haunted us.

William Hazlitt

Time to Forgive

[LOVE] KEEPS NO RECORD OF WRONG. *1 Corinthians 13:5*

An apologetic heart realizes its mistakes and understands its responsibility in a love relationship. It's willing to make amends, eager to ask for forgiveness, and anxious to reconcile. Love is a journey of humbleness mixed with regret and seasoned with sorrow. Forgiveness is a necessary and inevitable maturing step, which builds a foundation for growth and commitment.

Forgiveness is the ultimate expression of love. It can make bitterness sweet and transform a storm into a rainbow. This language of love is sometimes challenging to learn, but its rewards are healing and life-changing.

Dave Davidson

Love is the true means by which the world is enjoyed.

Thomas Traherne

Love is a seasoned spice becoming sweeter when mixed with forgiveness.

Dave Davidson

Love is an act of endless forgiveness, a tender look which becomes a habit.

Peter Ustinov

Love is for fools wise enough to take a chance.

Amy Grant, Wayne Kirkpatrick, & Michael W. Smith

Love is the adaptation and cooperation of toothpaste tube-squeezing methods.

Hugh Myrrh

LOVE IS RENUNCIATION OF
ONE'S PERSONAL COMFORT.

Leo Tolstoy

Love is the heart's immortal thirst to be
completely known and all forgiven.
Henry Van Dyke

Love is never missing a chance
to add a bit of sunshine in someone's life.
Diane Gammon

Love is not getting, but giving.
Henry Van Dyke

Sharing Heart

Since I have you in my heart . . . all of you share in God's grace with me.

Philippians 1:7

Two hearts find many ways to share love, whether through secrets or stories before untold. A sharing heart is willing to talk for hours on the phone or spend a long evening on a porch swing just for listening.

Correspondence becomes an essential ingredient preserving a relationship and nourishing it through distance and time. Writing letters and notes of adoration can be the extra spice in romancing any relationship. Gifts, whenever and whatever they are, always nurture love.

A sharing heart embraces and cherishes nature's offerings as if it were made for only two in full appreciation. Lakeshores hold new meaning, flowers emit enlightening fresh scents, and the moon seems to shine just for a selfish romantic conversation piece.

Dave Davidson

ART IS THE UNCEASING EFFORT TO COMPETE WITH THE BEAUTY
OF FLOWERS — AND NEVER SUCCEEDING.

Marc Chagall

Love is to communicate
to the other that you are all
for him, that you will never
fail him or let him down when
he needs you, but that you will
always be standing by with all
the necessary encouragements.

Ashley Montague

Love is above
all, the gift of
oneself.

Jean Anouilh

Love is
sensational,
but not senseless.
Love is vulnerable,
but not irresponsible.
Love is innocent,
but never lacks respect.
Love is romantic,
thriving best in reality.
Love is defenseless,
protecting the best within us.
Love is a way of happiness,
but not its exclusive avenue.

Dave Davidson

LOVE IS SPACE AND TIME
MEASURED BY THE HEART.
Marcel Proust

LOVE IS THE FAIREST AND MOST
PROFITABLE GUEST A REASONABLE
CREATURE CAN ENTERTAIN.
Richard Role

LOVE IS A LITTLE HAVEN OF REFUGE
FROM THE WORLD.
Bernard A. Russell

LOVE IS THE ENCHANTED DAWN
OF EVERY HEART.
Alphonse de Lamartine

45

Fragrance of Flowers

PLEASING IS THE FRAGRANCE OF YOUR PERFUMES. *Song of Solomon 1:3*

What is it about flowers that attract us to glare and gaze, to inhale the fragrance of their beauty? Perhaps we realize that in its delicate stature, the colorful petals are with us just days longer than a sunset's canvas or a rainbow's fading. Or is it the awareness of seed cultivated over time to produce such beauty that takes us in?

If it is a single flower, one may have to come close to appreciate its aroma. If huddled together in a garden, the fragrance can wisp a nearby couple over with its romantic scent. Whatever the attraction and whatever the hold, flowers are and will be nature's honorary gift of expressing love.

Dave Davidson

A rose is a rose is a rose.

Gertrude Stein

Love is something like the clouds that were

in the sky before the sun came out.

You cannot touch the clouds,

you know; but you feel the rain

and know how glad the flowers

and the thirsty earth are to have

it after a hot day.

You cannot touch love either,

but you feel the sweetness that

it pours into everything.

Annie Sullivan

When you brought the roses,
I felt something
Stir in me that I thought
was dead Forever.   *Frank D. Gilroy*

Love is
the affinity of intimacy,
the rhapsody of ecstasy,
and the tenderness
of sensuousness.

Dave Davidson

51

wild wild wild

overflowing hues from a passionate field
        with wild weeds
and their wild seeds . . .

        mixed with wild
yet mild daisies – colorful-sounding blue bells
and wild pink roses from the north

what's left is white baby's breath
intertwined with a wooden fence
vine accent

capturing a backyard's divinely designed
        fine bouquet
fit for a country queen

Dave Davidson

Kissed by Heaven

LET HIM KISS ME WITH THE KISSES OF HIS MOUTH —
FOR YOUR LOVE IS MORE DELIGHTFUL THAN WINE. *Song of Solomon 1:2*

Many look for love that is true and long lasting. What does it take to fall in love with someone? How can it become a "forever love"?

When we experience true love, it is a foretaste of heaven. God created love and demonstrated His own love for us by the sacrificial gift of His Son on the cross. He chose to reach down from heaven and love us completely and perfectly.

God's love created the standard by which we are to love one another. It is not a selfish love, but rather one that is unconditional and sometimes undeserved. It is a love grounded in faith and commitment. It is a love that can form a strong bond of faith and trust . . . a "forever love."

Dan Davidson

53

Love is that two solitudes protect
and touch and greet each other.

Rainer M. Rilke

To **love** and win **is** the best thing.
To love and lose, the next best.

William M. Thackeray

LOVE IS TO BELIEVE, TO HOPE, TO KNOW
— A TASTE OF HEAVEN BELOW.

Adapted from Edmund Waller

Love is

an image of God. . .
the living essence of
the divine nature which
beams full of all goodness.

Martin Luther

Love is a symbol of eternity.
It wipes out all sense of time,
destroying all memory of a
beginning and all fear of an end.

Anna Louise de Stael

55

Virtuous Vows

[Love] always trusts.   *1 Corinthians 13:7*

*W*edding vows are considered sacred. They represent a covenant relationship and godly union in spirit. The Bible tells us that where two are joined together, they will become one flesh. The mystery of this marriage union reflects our relationship with God himself.

*T*he Bible presents a metaphor with Christ as a groom and His church as a bride. In heaven, Christ and His church will come together in a wedding banquet and feast to celebrate a reunion of love and commitment for eternity. God invites each one of us to become a part of His kingdom. He has already revealed His wedding vows in His Word as part of godly promises and covenant. As a man and woman are united in marriage, the promises and vows made to each other have a sacred foundation found in heaven.   *Dan Davidson*

Love is the strange bewilderment which overtakes one person on account of another person.

James Thurber & E.B. White

Love is what you've been through with somebody.

James Thurber

LOVE IS BORN WITH THE PLEASURE OF

LOOKING AT EACH OTHER; IT IS FED

WITH THE NECESSITY OF SEEING

EACH OTHER; IT IS

CONCLUDED WITH THE

IMPOSSIBILITY OF

SEPARATION.

José Martí y Perez

LOVE IS THE BLINDING

REVELATION THAT

SOME OTHER BEING CAN BE

MORE IMPORTANT

TO LOVE THAN HE IS TO HIMSELF.

J.V. Casserley

Romantic

love is

a long-lasting battery

that needs regular recharging.

Ironically, dim lighting is a

great recharging method.

Dave Davidson

Love is a mutual admiration
society consisting of but two members . . .
the one whose love is less intense
will become president.

Joseph Mayer

Love is supreme and unconditional.

Duke Ellington

LOVE IS A RARE OPPORTUNITY AND WHEN THAT

LOVE IS SOMEHOW PARTED, IT'S SOMETHING DEEP DOWN

INSIDE THAT WANTS JUST A REMINDER,

A SLICE OF MEMORY, A POSSESSION.

Unknown

Love is hoping true romance
finds true commitment.

Dave Davidson

Love is all we have,
the only way
that each
can help
the other.

Euripides

Joy of Love

LOVE . . . ALWAYS HOPES. *1 Corinthians 13:7*

Joy is the flower of happiness, the scent of gladness, and an expression of love itself. A heart overjoyed and in love dances to the rhythm of life. It's the honeymoon of the heart becoming intoxicated, invigorated, and overwhelming. For a heart in love that hopes and expresses pure joy shares many benefits safely, securely, and with mutual satisfaction.

This joy may arrive via the lips by a smile, a kiss, or a kind compliment shared to express adoration. It can burst forth at a long-awaited reunion, a spontaneous surprise during a date, or by an unexpected gift which encapsulates recent affection.

Dave Davidson

Love is

a butterfly which,
when pursued is just
beyond your grasp, but if
you will sit down quietly,
it may alight upon you.

Nathaniel Hawthorne

Love is what melts winter with
the warmth of a spring kiss.

Dave Davidson

63

Love is sharing an intimate secret
in front of a fireplace crackling,
with two mugs of hot chocolate
in a romantic winter scene.

Dave Davidson

EVERY GARDENER KNOWS THAT UNDER
THE CLOAK OF WINTER LIES A MIRACLE.

Barbara Winkler

Hope, patience, and work —
these are the three graces of spring.

Ruth Shaw Ernst

It is the month of June,
   The month of leaves and roses,
      When pleasant sights salute the eyes
         And pleasant scents the noses.

Nathaniel Parker Willis

Love **is** a fruit in season at all times,
and within reach of every hand.

Mother Teresa

A heart kissed is an impression. It's a touching of souls, a brush with intimacy, a taste of delight. A kiss is a merging of two hearts fluttering, pounding on the very same beat when lips meet. This synchronicity happens only when you kiss, for each heart picks up the tempo, the count, the meter of the other heart like radar, and simultaneously strikes the same chord.

This refreshing note is in honor of a loved one's heart, leading to other melodies, harmonies in lipstick duets. A kiss is a contact, a conviction, a connection. Whether fireworks of a first kiss explode the sky far from the Fourth of July or a continuous kiss contract is exchanged, kissing is the doorway to romance and the living room of love itself. It can be passion's moment with flocculating degrees, temperatures, and variable humidity.

A kiss resembles a pair of pliers connecting mutually compatible wires. A kiss is no different than checking the mailbox and finding an awaited package. Experiencing a kiss's intricacies rivals the discovery of a rare shooting star on a clear August evening. A kiss is the enshrouding of newness or the maintenance of a promise. It's a physical debut, which stars the very part of the body that speaks words of love.

Dave Davidson

EVERY SEASON IS DIFFERENT IN THE GARDEN, AND ONE OF GARDENING'S

GREATEST APPEALS IS THE CHANGES IN THE FORMS, COLORS,

AND PERFUMES THAT MARK THE PASSAGE OF THE YEAR IN A

DYNAMIC AND CONTINUALLY INTERESTING MANNER.

Stefan Buczacki

Love is

swinging and swaying,

cuddling cozy together

on a net mesh hammock

allowing room to breathe

in the summer breeze.

Dave Davidson

Spring is a place
for new beginnings,
for budding of blossoms,
for the planting of flowers
and for the anticipation
of its unique warmth.
It signifies the end of
a cold, dry, dark era,
the end of winter's
long-lasting length
of lonely nights.

Becca Lynn

69

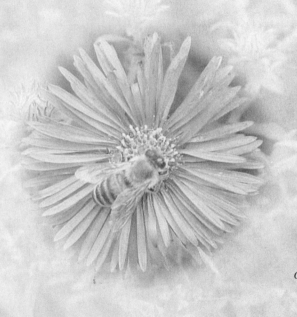

Life
is
the
flower
for
which
love is
the
honey.

Oliver Wendell
Holmes

LOVE IS SOMETHING ETERNAL;

THE ASPECT MAY CHANGE,

BUT NOT THE ESSENCE.

Aristotle

Love is giving away umbrellas
then getting caught in refreshing rain
while showers drench you all over.

Dave Davidson

Love is

a wedding day
in May,
a honeymoon
in June
and never doubting
why ever
in July.

Dave Davidson

Journey for Life

Love . . . always perseveres. *1 Corinthians 13:6–7*

*L*ove is a journey that can be finished in a season or last a lifetime. Infatuation is here for a day, but tomorrow may fade away. Persevering love prepares itself for years of commitment, devotion, and faithfulness.

*O*n the journey of love, commitment is the spark that renews and revitalizes. Devotion is the seed that nourishes and supports. Faithfulness is the promise that sustains and strengthens.

*F*or love to last a lifetime, it must grow stronger during the trials of life, learning to persevere with hope. Through the ups and downs of life, the time we invest in a relationship develops a persevering love. Fasten your seatbelts for the ride of your life . . . a journey of love.

Dan Davidson

73

LOVE IS
FULL OF EMOTION;
YOU EXPERIENCE
A WONDERFUL FEELING,
LIKE A TRIP THROUGH THE OCEAN
OR A VOYAGE THROUGH OUR LIVING.
ONE DAY A WAVE TOLD ME:
"IF YOUR LOVE IS TRUE,
NOT EVEN THE STRONGEST SEA
WOULD SEPARATE YOU TWO."

Pat from Barranquilla

In the soul of each heart
a reservoir of love resides,
a river ready to spring forward,
a waterfall ready to descend . . .
to where love abides.

Dave Davidson

Where we **love is** home,
home that our feet may leave,
but not our hearts.

Victor Hugo

Love is to commit
oneself without guarantee,
to give oneself completely
in the hope that our love
will produce love in
the loved person.

Erich Fromm

Real
love is a pilgrimage.
It happens when there is no strategy,
but it is very rare because most
people are strategists.

Anita Brookner

Love is
eternal
    and enduring,
constant
    and continuous,
endearing
    and everlasting.

Dave Davidson

77

Love is a journey of sensational senses.

Dave Davidson

Brothers Dan & Dave Davidson share the same mission statement in the acronym T.I.M.E. — To Teach, Inspire, Motivate, and Encourage. They have written over 20 books together including *The Fragrance of Christmas*, *A Cup of Devotion With God*, *Surviving Temptation Island*, and *Spirit of America Lives*.

Both brothers record verbatim Scripture songs for PoetTree.com and both are inspirational speakers. Dan is a chiropractor in Virginia and Dave is a photographer in Iowa — DavesPhotography.com. Dan and his wife, Kimberly, have three children. Dave and his wife, Joan, have two children.

For more on romance and love visit FragranceOfLove.com
For a current list of their books
and free online resources visit
DanDavidson.com & DaveDavidson.com
They can be reached at
Dan@DanDavidson.com & Dave@DaveDavidson.com

Other books by Dan & Dave Davidson

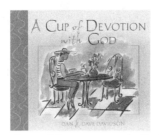

A Cup of Devotion with God
0-89221-426-0
$5.99

The Fragrance of Christmas
0-89221-425-2
$5.99

Available at Christian bookstores nationwide